# Brown Fox Tricks ...rk

Written by Alison Hawes
Illustrated by Richard Watson

Brown Fox is at the market.

She chats to Stork. "Join me and I will cook you this corn."

They return to Fox's den.

Fox thinks of a trick as she starts to cook.

Fox grins and tips the corn into flat dishes.

Fox slurps up her corn.

But Stork frowns.
She can not get at her food.

Stork is cross but she keeps it to herself.

Next morning, Stork is in her garden.

She chats to Brown Fox. "Join me and I will cook you this fish."

Stork grins and tips the fish into long thin jars.

Stork slurps up her fish.
But Fox frowns. She can not get at her food!

Brown Fox growls at Stork.

But Stork just grins.

Trick me, and I will trick you!